The Secret Millionaire Mindset:

Success strategies and practices that will Bring you Wealth

By

David K. Berry

Table of Content

Introduction

As many individuals have noticed, "Achievement leaves hints." If you need to make exceptional progress in the approaching year, concentrate on the specialists, do what they do, and alter their strategies to suit what is going on. It's simple!
I've known individuals who brought in some cash, yet I've never known anybody who got rich without analyzing their qualities, needs, and convictions. Begin with your qualities.
No one can hit an objective they can't see. Characterize your results and set clear, feasible outcomes ahead of time. Know what "achievement" seems to be! Have quantifiable, explicit results, and discover that you will accomplish them!

An immense motivation behind why individuals can't draw in abundance is that they don't comprehend the reason for how and why they need to become rich. They meander through existence without bearing. They burn through the majority of their lives in wretchedness. To move forward, consequently, you want to have A reason throughout everyday life.

The law of direction says that assuming you find your motivation, you can show abundance, achievement, and joy. Without a feeling of direction, it is difficult to be content. It is by chasing your motivation that you gain bliss and abundance. Assuming that even if you become rich, for no reason, you can't achieve joy.
When you put stock in overflow, you can show your fantasies through the general rule that good energy attracts good. The pattern of good following good can draw into you what you accept. With an overflow mindset, you see potential open doors all over the place. However, before taking on an overflow mindset, you have probably been conveying the stuff of a 'shortage' attitude. You convey feelings of hatred for slip-ups of the past; feelings of resentment against individuals you never again recollect. To empower you to embrace an overflow mindset, you need to excuse yourself for such previous oversights.

There are strong powers behind cash that make the collection of it conceivable among individuals. Consequently, drawing in cash is neither mysterious nor the result of science.

With this attractive power, anybody can draw in the sort of cash he wants.

As per the pattern of good following good working in the universe, you will undoubtedly draw what you need into your life.

Since people are living magnets, they will undoubtedly draw into themselves individuals, circumstances, and conditions that are at one with their predominant contemplations.

The pattern of energy attracting similar energy is one of the extraordinary laws of the universe. It says that all you own throughout everyday life, you have drawn to yourself on account of how you think.

You can completely change yourself since you can have an impact on how you think. In this way, your attitude decides when and the amount you can acquire.

At the point when you foster a passionate longing for cash and consider it constantly, you set up a power field of close-to-home energy that draws in individuals, and thoughts and opens doors to you to assist you with achieving your motivation.

In this way, your street to drawing in abundance to yourself starts with your reception of another example of thought.

Here are different techniques for drawing favorable luck for yourself. One, go on an undertaking to grasp cash. You can never draw in or hold what you don't have any idea about. Which is the reason an absence of comprehension of cash will lead you to destitution.

Thusly, you should put resources into assets that will enable you on the most proficient method to deal with cash. Cash is a dependable worker and when conveyed handily, it will create riches.

Two, mind your words. You must be rich as you articulate. Along these lines, watch what you say.

The general rule that good energy attracts good commands us to meaningfully have an impact on our perspective, which means what you say. The force of confirming the right words over your life can't be over-accentuated.

Asserting your desires, despite your current conditions, is exceptionally successful for acquiring what you need. Begin avowing your points day to day, and in a matter of seconds, things will start to adjust in understanding your desires.

From currently, begin certifying that you are well off and before this year runs out, you will end up being a rich man.

Three, strip yourself of self-restricting convictions. For instance, accepting that each rich man became rich falsely is a self-restricting conviction.

Attempt to dissect and cast off regrettable convictions about cash.

Four, make a move on any drive, hindquarters, or instinct on how you can become rich. Continuously follow up on your thoughts, since cash likes speed.

Five, be hopeful. Continuously anticipate that best of luck should happen to you. By so thinking, you will draw in karma to yourself.

There is power in assumption, for what you expect becomes reality. Anticipate that great should come in your direction and it will work out so.

Chapter1

The mystery of wealth

For what reason do we accept that when you rake in some serious cash, that implies you are rich? What's the significance here? The Dictionary characterizes rich as "having a lot of cash or resources; well off," yet we should contemplate that briefly. How can you spend your cash? Since you might be bringing in a lot of cash doesn't guarantee to mean you are rich.

A typical snare of big-time salary workers is that even though they might be getting a huge load of cash, they are likewise burning through a large chunk of change. There is this thought that they need to flaunt their cash and partake in their cash, which frequently prompts overspending.
Individuals frequently don't understand that as opposed to spending your cash as it comes in, you can get your cash working for you through ventures, then procuring automated revenue on those speculations. At the point when you get your cash working for yourself and have your cash producing considerably more cash, that is a perfect balance.

The tricks of the trade to becoming rich, in no specific request, are:

1. Try not to spend your cash on depreciable resources

The biggest depreciable resource individuals spend the most cash on our vehicles. It is enticing to buy a delightfully marked, completely stacked extravagance vehicle that will cost you nearly six figures, while perhaps not more. In any case, that cash would be better contributed and pay you a profit from that venture.

2. Never spend more cash than you make

It's enticing to stay aware of the Joneses and burn through cash on contraptions, extravagance things that don't hold worth, and "stuff" that you don't require, however assuming you are spending more cash than you are making, that amasses obligation, and obligation costs cash to convey. Your cash would better serve you contributed where it pays a return.

3. Building interest is the eighth miracle of the world

At the point when you put away your cash and are acquiring revenue on top of revenue, your cash develops at a remarkable rate. Nonetheless, the converse is valid when you are conveying obligation. You pay cash to have that obligation at a dramatic rate too, and it gobbles up your cash rapidly.

4. Put resources into monetary schooling

At the point when you put resources into yourself and figure out how to deal with your cash, that profit from the venture will be inconceivable, given that you execute what you've realized.

There will be an exceptional yield on speculation into the indefinite future when you utilize the monetary abilities you have figured out how to deal with your cash better.

5. Contribute and follow your total assets

Track your total assets is the most ideal way to gauge your riches. Your total assets,the entirety of your resources (what you own) less the entirety of your liabilities (what you owe). The higher your total assets number is, the more extravagant you are. Your abundance lies in the resources you own, like ventures, resources investment properties, and anything you own that holds an incentive for quite a while.

6. Your total assets lie in your way of behaving around cash

How you spend, save, and deal with your cash will decide how well off you are or will turn into. One of the ongoing ideas among the most well-off individuals is that they are not conspicuous about it. They have amazing measures of cash however are not regularly seen traveling on the most costly yachts, wearing garish garments, or carrying on with an extreme way of life.

7. Design an arrangement for progress

Having an arrangement is by a wide margin the main mystery of all. An objective without an arrangement is only a wish, so for you to accomplish your monetary objectives, you want to design your ventures. At the point when you plan and guide out your objectives, it's simpler to gauge your outcomes against your objectives and consider yourself responsible. Having an arrangement makes your objectives noteworthy.

The primary concern is if you are not offering your monetary arrangement the consideration that it needs to create your financial wellbeing, the time has come to do as such. The profit from that venture of time, cash, and energy will duplicate itself throughout the long term and will probably be the best speculation you have made for yourself as well as your monetary future.

8. Get rich gradually.

The way to extraordinary abundance is to limit pay while augmenting your resources. Pay is burdened. Pay gets spent, contemplate every one of the vehicles, boats, jewels, and houses individuals with tremendous earnings like to purchase!
Putting resources into resources that are difficult to spend (structures, stocks and bonds, collectible workmanship, and so forth) makes abundance that isn't burdened, and isn't spent on a relaxed drive.

9. Cover heaps of charges.
No, I'm not looking at paying more than you owe, however, pay each penny the law requires. Rich

people don't wrangle over nickels and dimes, they contribute to making millions!

If you can lawfully stay away from charges, do as such! Utilize the law for your potential benefit when you can. However, shuffling the books to conceal pay or save a couple of bucks, burns through your time, squanders your energy, makes dread getting found out, and makes you modest. Try not to make it happen!

Chapter2

Life reason

Your life reason comprises the focal spurring points of your life, the reasons you get up toward the beginning of the day.

For certain individuals, the intention is associated with employment significant, fulfilling work. Certain individuals might find their motivation communicated in this multitude of parts of life.

The reason will be interesting for everybody; what you distinguish as your way might be not the same as others. Likewise, your motivation can move and change throughout life in light of the advancing needs and variances of your encounters.

Questions that might come up when you think about your life design are:

Who am I?
Where do I have a place?
When do I feel satisfied?

Your life object is your commitment
Certain individuals have a reluctant outlook on chasing after their life reason since they stress that it seems like a self-serving or narrow-minded mission. Notwithstanding, the genuine object is tied in with perceiving your gifts and utilizing them to add to the world whether those gifts are playing wonderful music for others to appreciate, assisting companions

with taking care of issues, or carrying more euphoria into the existence of people around you.

How life reason develops
Inquiries regarding life reason might emerge out of the blue throughout everyday life, except you might see that they are particularly predominant during seasons of progress or emergency. for instance, a vocation or instructive change, individual misfortune, or significant distance move.

Our life should be visible as a nautilus that adds new chambers to its shell as it develops and needs more space. Similarly, as individuals develop into an alternate period of life, their old chambers can feel squeezed. They start to ask how they might extend their space.

Moving into new chambers opens up the way for additional opportunities to arise, permitting our life reason to advance. In any case, this can likewise provoke physical, mental, profound, and otherworldly changes and, surprisingly, some of the time a tumultuous period as we pose new inquiries.

Starting from the very beginning, logicians and ordinary citizens the same have considered the possibility of a "day-to-day existence reason."
In any case, what characterizes one's life reason? Furthermore, what should yours be?

In the least complex terms, a daily existence object is your explanation (or purposes behind) getting up in the first part of the day. Genuine reason can direct your choices.

It will impact your way of behaving and assist you with focusing on objectives to account for the main thing.

Reason can offer an internal compass… and make meaning. For certain individuals, design is associated with a job significant, fulfilling work.

Old Greek classicists considered it a "telos," or a definitive objective of life. They accepted that a daily existence reason ought to be one's focal spotlight on their process through time on the planet.

Present-day masterminds conceptualize it as that what they were intended to do or be… what they were made for.

However, you like to consider it, having a thought of your more prominent point in life makes consistently more huge and valuable. It permits you to outfit your energy into an option that could be greater than just yourself.

Everybody has various abilities and gifts that make them incredible. and finding the opportunity to dissect what you succeed at can provide you further guidance to what you can call your life reason.

Journaling is what makes the biggest difference to you.
Innovative journaling has many demonstrated medical advantages. From recording your insane dreams to observing intriguing blossoms you've seen that day, it allows you passed on the mind an opportunity to put itself out there, or your right cerebrum time to get a handle on the day. Consistency is significant. If you pick a story approach, you give your friends and family an

important record and device to look into the everyday existence of your loved ones.

At the point when you select an imaginative methodology, like a verse or portraying, you can get a brief look into your inner mind and the subjects of your life.

Either strategy works… and a large number of the world's best personalities work on journaling.

You can likewise begin involving your diary as a device to carry out your life reason. Everything from certifications, motivating statements, or an everyday plan for the day will want to assist you with exploring the waters of heading out toward your fantasies.

Composing a day-to-day existence reason explanation

Is it true or not that you are feeling courageous?

Provided that this is true, plunk down and record a statement of purpose of the motivation behind your life. You may be shocked by your thought process!

For your most memorable draft, don't place a lot of thought into it and let the sensation of what you need to most communicate move through you. Be consistent with yourself and don't be bashful; you don't need to share it on the off chance that you would rather not. Afterward, reconsider it and sort through it. Work out an individual declaration on the off chance that you need to. Allow the composed word to motivate you to do more noteworthy things and focus on the most striking subtleties.

Try not to contemplate it, all things considered. You can have a little or reduced reason, like turning into a veggie lover. Or on the other hand, you might find something more noteworthy, such as turning into a common freedoms dissident or revealing a melodic ability.

Take what you gain from this activity and use it to settle on far superior decisions for your life.

Track down great writing or media to help your new vision, and on the off chance that you are truly feeling roused, volunteer or take classes to move along.

Expressing to another person what makes the biggest difference

Discussing things with a humane audience assists our brains with handling what's happening in our life.

Indeed, even the most common way of standing by listening to ourselves talk can assist with making what's happening "genuine" and, all the more significantly, provide us with certain thoughts of the smart move moves toward initiate.

Track down a confided face to face and converse with them about it. The gigantic recuperating properties of telling somebody your mystery wants will continuously reveal insight into those sides of your life and give you trust and an alternate point of view.

Envisioning what is most significant in their life and what might need.

Peering inside assists you with explaining what's significant and limiting interruptions.

For instance, if being solid is essential to you… you could change your eating routine, learn new recipes, or begin an everyday workout plan.

On the off chance that having a good time with your local area is an objective, you may be keeping watch for chances to meet new individuals.

Imagine what your ideal life would be like, and make strides consistently to accomplish it!
Take a full breath, light a candle, and shut your eyes. Unwind and think: where might my life at any point go? What might I have? Where might I be? What might it seem like?

Presently, let yourself work out what an ideal day would be like. Let your creative mind go wild. Where might you travel? What might you eat? What presents could you purchase for your loved ones? You understand. Presently, ground yourself, and let yourself sort out a practical method for adjusting yourself to the existence decisions you could make to more encapsulate that way of life.

It's simpler than it sounds, and you can be stunned by any means of the assets that uncover themselves to you when you're open and prepared to get them or when you go out there and make a move.

Individuals from varying backgrounds benefit from the force of representation. From CEOs to rudimentary educators, strolling yourself through the essential strides to your eye helps guide you to procedures or apparatuses for a superior life.

It tends to be anything from a powerful tone to an exceptional spot in nature from which you draw motivation.

Chapter 3

Change your reasoning example

Quite possibly the main thing treatment has shown me is that changing your thinking examples can change as long as you can remember. We've fully grown with specific idea designs engrained in us, given what we've realized, noticed, and acquired. Some are more good, similar to "It feels better to help others". However, some can be weakening, similar to "I need to succeed or I am not commendable".

These idea designs are real brain associations in our cerebrums that have been fortified over the long haul. So it isn't difficult to change them. It resembles retraining a muscle. It requires investment and exertion, yet when you do, man is it worth the effort!

The most vital phase in changing an idea design you've had for what seems like forever is just to begin remembering it. Intermittently we think in a specific way without knowing it. In the first place, simply take a stab at recognizing the minutes when those thought designs kick in. For instance, I've as of late acknowledged how much strain I put on myself to do everything right. I'll see minutes when I get focused over my day and acknowledge they're frequently made by this perspective. Indeed, even something as basic as getting in the right line at the supermarket. I'll see a slight sensation of uneasiness and understand it's originating from this thought that I can do nothing off-base.

Yet rather than disgracing myself for having these contemplations, I attempt to recognize them just. I'll simply see when they are there. I don't attempt to transform them immediately, however, absolutely getting in the example of recognizing them is fundamental for the subsequent stage. It additionally abnormally causes me to feel less restless. Naming the idea or feeling that is happening in my mind can free some from the uneasiness related to that idea.

1: UNDERSTAND WHERE IT COMES FROM

It's so essential to see precisely the exact thing these idea designs mean, where you learned them, and what you understand concerning them. When we analyze them, we can understand how irrational or unreasonable that perspective is. This can be generally gainful with a specialist, yet you can positively do it all alone or with a companion too.

You truly should simply keep asking yourself inquiries, similar to "For what reason do you feel as such?", "What others in your life maintain this viewpoint?", "Who showed you this perspective (straightforwardly or indirectly)?", "What is your earliest memory of reasoning this way"?, "What would occur on the off chance that you didn't hold this view?", and so on. Questions like these can help uncover such a huge amount about yourself. Furthermore, when you get a superior comprehension of why you figure a specific way, modifying that perspective can be simpler.

2: CREATE AN ALTERNATIVE RESPONSE

When you get some margin to thoroughly consider where these idea designs come from (which can require hours or even years), the following stage is to make an elective reaction. Attempt and think of something you could say in your mind to supplant the point of view you're attempting to change. For instance, with the ludicrous measure of tension I put on myself, the elective reaction I concocted is: "You don't need to be great." It's something I'll rehash to myself in those minutes when I can hear those old idea designs coming through. It might sound basic, but it can truly help as long as you think of another reaction that genuinely addresses you.

3: PRACTICE AND BE PATIENT

From how I've spread this out, it might seem like you simply go through the three stages, and afterward, you're fixed. Indeed, it doesn't exactly work that way. Significantly altering how you think requires some investment and exertion. It's the same as muscle memory, retraining your muscles resemble retraining your mind. So show restraint toward yourself. Allow yourself to remain in Step 1 however long you want, or rehash Step 1 when you're simply feeling too restless to even consider paying attention to a substitute reaction. What's more, assuming you understand after some time that the other reaction you concocted isn't working, permit yourself to investigate another choice. Give yourself the existence to permit this figured example to change as the need might arise.

At the point when you are attempting to change a default thinking propensity or conduct, it is very much like figuring out how to drive on the opposite roadside. It's a diligent effort.

Whether you drive on the left or the right, it is challenging to reshape your thought process.

It should be extremely alarming for unfamiliar drivers who are accustomed to driving on the right-hand roadside coming to spots like New Zealand and changing by driving on the left-hand side.

I followed your run-of-the-mill white travel industry camper van once, and as it came up to a traffic circle, it turned right rather than left.

I pondered where in the world it was going as I saw it on the opposite side of the crossing point.

At the point when you have driven on one roadside, for your entire life, it turns into a profoundly instilled speculation propensity. So profound that it pauses for a minute by the second fixation and works to ensure you don't return to old patterns. It's a default thinking propensity.

Junkies find it unquestionably hard to change since they need to go against each draw of reasoning and feeling that would have them slip once more into the old trench.

In addition to those with habits, issues find it hard to change; we as a whole do.

Frequently we don't change since it's excessively troublesome, a lot of exertion is required.
We won't attempt to change until we are completely persuaded that the ongoing thought process and acting are perilous.

Figuring out how to rethink your reasoning permits you to see circumstances according to alternate points of view so you can go with additional educated choices. You can work on rethinking your considerations whenever utilizing basic methods. On the off chance that your thinking designs are adversely influencing your psychological well-being, it tends to be useful to figure out how to rethink those thought designs fully supported by a specialist. Here are a few stages you can take on the off chance that you need to rethink your reasoning.

The most important phase in reexamining your thinking designs is building a careful consciousness of the contemplations you are having. Noticing your contemplations can be precarious, yet gets simpler with training. Ask yourself everything that accounts you are saying to yourself about the circumstance you're in. Investigate how the various kinds of considerations you have can cause you to feel contrastingly contingent upon the idea. It can assist with getting to know normal idea designs that can cause issues for individuals. Certain individuals find care practices supportive while they're attempting to tune into their viewpoints.

Seeing your considerations without passing judgment on them is significant. Recollect that you don't need to feel terrible for having a thought, and you are in charge of how you answer your considerations.

One-sided thought designs provide you with a mistaken perspective on your general surroundings. This implies that your considerations about a circumstance probably won't be mirroring what's occurring. Whenever you have distinguished a thought, contrast it with the current realities of the circumstance. Inquire as to whether there is any proof supporting the idea, or any proof that doesn't uphold it.

On the off chance that you can't track down a lot of proof for an idea, or on the other hand on the off chance that there are things that go against what you're thinking, these are signs to relinquish that idea. For instance, assuming you are investing energy with your companion and they are a lot calmer than expected, you could imagine that they think that you are exhausted. You should seriously think about the way that they are by and large calm as proof that upholds this idea. Then again, the way that they are your companion and that they are as yet investing energy with you and haven't returned home yet are signs that your thinking probably won't be precise. The following stage is to investigate a few different clarifications.Whenever you have weighed up the proof for and against your idea, consider assuming there are elective contemplations that fit your circumstance better. Returning to the case of your companion being calmer than expected, one more clarification for this may be that they're recently drained, or that they are stressed over something inconsequential to you. You don't want to trust the elective idea immediately, yet over the long haul, getting into the propensity for considering different perspectives assists you with thinking all the more deftly and try not to stall out in one-sided thought designs. One-sided speculation examples can be difficult to perceive if you don't have the foggiest idea of what to search for. Many happen naturally, so you probably won't know you're having them. They can likewise be built up to such an extent that you probably won't understand you can transform them and accept that is the status quo. Assuming that you perceive that you're participating in a portion of these perspectives and they're adversely affecting your psychological well-being, it tends to be trying to change them all alone.

Chapter 4

Increment your Income

To save more cash for future objectives and incidental lavish expenditures, you might be prepared to roll out an improvement. Expanding your pay can decrease monetary tension, assist you with arriving at investment funds objectives and work on your general personal satisfaction. So how would you get that going? Peruse on for eight activities you can take today to help your pay.

1. Request a raise or reward

When did you last request a raise at work? Or then again would you say you are simply ready to be given one? Requesting a raise is an extraordinary methodology for how to effectively build your pay.

Be that as it may, you need to ensure you get everything done well. While intending to ask your supervisor for a raise, you really must plan to have the discussion.

Archive your achievements and honors at work. Make certain to feature explicit measurements and results to grandstand how your commitments and range of abilities have emphatically assisted the organization with meeting its goals. You'll be your publicity individual to put forth your defense.

On the off chance that a quick raise is unimaginable, don't surrender. You can ask your manager what it will take for you to receive that next pay increase or work reward.

Once more, utilize your previous presentation history to feature your history, and afterward work with your supervisor to define execution objectives for a future raise.

2. Find a superior paying line of work

Is a raise not in the cards at this moment? Was the raise you got sufficiently not? It very well may be an ideal opportunity to tidy off your resume and your Linkedin profile and begin searching for a superior paying position.

3. Find a part-time line of work

Seasonal work on the off chance that your timetable licenses are a truly incredible method for helping pay. Particularly on the off chance that a raise or a more lucrative occupation are not promptly accessible. Your temporary occupation doesn't need to be anything extravagant and it likewise doesn't need to be extremely durable.

You can choose to work part-time for a particular period or until you meet a specific monetary objective. Everything revolves around zeroing in on what you need to achieve by utilizing a seasonal task to assist you with speeding up your course of events.

With regards to working part-time, you must be aware of how you spend the additional cash you are procuring.

The last thing you need is to remove additional time from your rest or your family to work more hours and afterward have the cash get past you. Make certain to anticipate this pay in your financial plan.

4. Begin a minimal expense second job

Beginning a second job is the way to expand your pay while building a business. Essentially, it permits you to adapt what you are great at or adapt to something you have an interest in. Your part-time job could be something you set up during the night after work or at the end of the week.

Remember that with regards to developing your second job to productivity, you will show restraint. You could likewise have to master explicit business abilities like making a field-tested strategy, promoting, and business funds.

5. Clean up your home and sell your stuff

We live in a day and age where we are inclined to obtain more stuff than we truly need. Therefore, we in some cases end up with more than we truly need and a lot of unused stuff jumbling into our homes.

On the off chance that you are feeling such, cleaning up is smart. You can relinquish things that you never again need yet at the same time have to esteem and procure some additional pay.

This cash can gigantically affect accomplishing your monetary objectives. Where you can sell rapidly and effectively incorporate Facebook Marketplace, Etsy, Poshmark, and eBay.

6. Cut expenses at every possible opportunity

It's amazing how much cash you can squander on subtle costs like unused memberships, squandered food, high service bills, and so on. Track down ways of cutting your financial plan and lowering costs to rapidly support pay.

For example, attempt these stunts for bringing down your electric bill, look for less expensive protection, and do dinner prep so you don't get take-out when you don't want to cook.

7. Bring in cash from your leisure activities

Bringing in cash from your leisure activities is how to build your pay while having a great time! On the off chance that you appreciate creating you can sell those charming things, you make on destinations like Etsy. Or on the other hand on the off chance that you have a green thumb, you can sell blossoms and plants at a neighborhood rancher's market.

Anything your energy is without a doubt you can bring in cash from it! Utilizing the side interests you love doing is an extraordinary method for supporting pay rapidly.

8. Make automated revenue

Recurring, automated revenue is how to persistently acquire additional pay. The best thing about automated revenue is after the underlying set-up or work you keep on acquiring from it. For instance, putting resources into the securities exchange, procuring sovereignties from a distributed book, and investment properties are ways of making recurring, automated revenue.

So dynamic pay is where you "effectively" work a side gig or occupation however automated revenue is where you procure long after the work is finished.

Utilize these tips to rapidly expand your pay

As you find additional ways to build your pay, be certain that you set the right aims for your extra profit. You would rather not burn through your time or the expanded pay you procure, particularly in the wake of really buckling down for that cash.

Focus on setting up an arrangement ahead of time to take care of your obligation, set aside more cash, increment your speculations, and towards your different objectives.

Chapter5

Abundance Attraction

Assuming you think bringing in cash is troublesome, particularly in these fierce times, stand by till you attempt to make it last. It takes every one of one's monetary insight and endeavors to save, contribute and assist it with development. All the more so for celebs and stars, who are wont to produce bountiful measures of abundance and make awkward portfolios. Impeded by the absence of monetary aptitude and scarcity of time, they frequently wind up entrusting their abundance to wasteful abundance chiefs, or more awful, corrupt ones. At different times, supported by progress and false trust in their capacities to oversee cash, they take wrong financial planning choices. Then, at that point, there's the exciting entanglement of influence, which makes them accept their cash will last forever. For these and a few different reasons, the world promotes a not insignificant rundown of VIPs who have procured untold riches, just to lose everything. Some have taken in their illustrations and recuperated, while others neglect to do as such. Notwithstanding the incongruence in the quantum of abundance made by such celebs and the typical salaried expert, there are monetary examples to be advanced by all.

Cash, to some degree, is something we as a whole length to make. As business people, genuine achievement accompanies the capacity to get abundance going, and can call it in voluntarily. While making abundance once may seem adequately like, the monetary achievement is additionally estimated by how we fabricate it. Without the capacity to hold that progress in our lives, we are right starting over from the beginning.
Project your brain back to the last time you encountered that snapshot of monetary achievement, whether it was winning an agreement or a PDA warning making you aware of your recently recharged bank balance. Assuming reproducing that second presently feels like it was down to dumb karma, then, at that point, you're in good company.
You held back nothing and showed the cash you wanted. Yet, to rehash it, one significant inquiry remains: Where did that want come from?
It is possible that you showed abundance from a position of need. At the end of the day, you were pursuing your "thought" of accomplishment since

you felt that something was absent. You were shooting in obscurity with no genuine point. The outcome? The outcome of a comparable sort will be rare again because you won't ever know where to track down it. Living plentifully can assist you with drawing in cash because your emphasis isn't on what's deficient. Where we place our consideration is how we make our world all things considered.

Nothing bad can be said about pursuing our fantasies. it's our drive as business visionaries. However, we frequently get so occupied by the curiosity of our end objective that we neglect to make a move in the correct manner (or even by any means). On the off chance that we continually consider our objectives something we need, we are preparing our psyches to consider them something to fear: the unexplored world.

Living bounteously can assist you with drawing in cash by placing these things into point of view.

You need to bring in cash, how much and why? You need to be better. how much weight would you like to lose, and why? You need the ideal relationship. what makes the ideal accomplice in your eyes, and why? By being ruthlessly legit with ourselves, we can begin to illustrate what that achievement resembles, and how we could approach arriving.

Conditions might change en route. You might encounter things on the excursion that make you question your life's account, and whether you are on the correct way by any stretch of the imagination. Above all, simply by making a move might we at any point track down the responses to these inquiries?

All in all, what might be living richly do for you to draw in cash, rather than simply pursuing it?

To begin with, we should pause for a minute to consider what we'd characterize as overflow. I like to contrast overflow with nature, the world's regular peculiarity that simply continues to give. At the point when you consider it, nature is likewise relentless. It will continuously figure out how to get by, long after people leave this world. Overflow is a relentless power. At last, it is the normal request of things.

Residing bounteously is tied in with knowing how to show accomplishment in your life, and live from a position of overflow.

This is all paying little heed to what it is you wish to get in your world. Without exemplifying overflow, we couldn't practically expect to partake in our prosperity reliably. To carry on with an existence with overflow is to work from a position of development, and not a position of constriction. However, what does everything truly mean?

With such a lot of dread and tension whirling around nowadays, you could contend that our profound state has been compromised now like never before previously. As the world keeps on closing itself away, sensations of uncertainty, fault, and disgrace just take steps to keep us away from arriving at our maximum capacity.

Through a progression of four key stages, you can open that bountiful life by separating those undetectable obstructions.

1 - Accept: the demonstration of tolerating liability regarding your activities. To begin with, we recognize the way that we are the creator of our stories. All that has occurred up until this point is a consequence of our decisions, both cognizant or oblivious. From here, we can pursue choices from a position of truth.

2 - Clear: the demonstration of the understanding you can't pursue fair decisions from a position of misrepresentation. It's tied in with being more present with ourselves to pursue the decisions adequately strong to influence genuine change. Is it safe to say that you are consistent with yourself right now?

3 - Gratitude: the demonstration of perceiving that all that we experience is a consequence of assumption. We're welcome to invite you in appreciation a whole lot sooner on our excursion. As the most impressive epitome of good assumption, feeling thankful for something ahead of time can be an impetus for change.

4 - Listen: the demonstration of mirroring that we are human. We pull back from the possibility of hairsplitting and regard the way that we will goof occasionally. This just empowers progress. At the point when we've become sidetracked, it's tied in with pulling ourselves back with beauty and self-esteem so we might keep on gaining ground.

While doing this, we should likewise regard the way that such change might be important for a drawn-out plan. Rome wasn't inherent a day, and neither should your vision be as a business person. Steady-minded individuals will win in the end; having dominated that energy, there's not a great explanation you can't be set forever.

Coming from a position of truth and a position of persistence is, consequently, key to making those little yet pivotal strides towards your objective. By figuring out how to live richly across all parts of your life, beneficial things will normally follow. Whether that be riches, well-being, or cheerful connections overflow prepares for boundless potential outcomes.

So whenever you're pursuing the possibility of progress, make a stride back and ask yourself: What is my meaning of progress? Really at that time might you at any point genuinely partake in a plentiful, happy, reason-driven presence — and all life's wealth you might find inside it.

Conclusion

Living with dread and stress restrains achievement. Stress and dread gobble up the confidence you should marshal to draw in abundance.

develop a mentality of appreciation. Be thankful and energetic about what you have. Karma and cash flourish in a mentality of appreciation and liberality.

The people who utilize their assets to help other people will themselves be honored by the Almighty consequently.

An otherworldly regulation asserts that the people who surrender end up getting to an ever-increasing extent, while the individuals who crowd wind up getting less. What you give returns to you in large numbers.

Cash is a power. It is a concentrated image of energy and power throughout everyday life. Like all powers in the universe, cash submits to specific widespread regulations or standards. By understanding those regulations and acting suitably, we gain extraordinary control over cash, empowering riches and flourishing to come to our direction.

The vast majority of us know about the significance of difficult work, assurance, and head to draw in cash. Be that as it may, there are likewise other, more covered up and inconspicuous ways of drawing in cash, riches, and thriving. At the point when followed, these techniques tend to right away draw in cash from apparently all of a sudden, resisting our ordinary thoughts of circumstances and logical results, and what is sensible and conceivable. Such abrupt and bountiful outcomes indicate the wondrous peculiarity of "life reaction" at work.

It is a fundamental law of life that everything whether it is an actual article or a person answers more prominent consideration. Cash is no exemption. The most effective way to concentrate entirely on cash is to represent it precisely and on time. Staying up with the latest records of cash is a strong component for unexpectedly drawing in a greater amount of it.

Like any power, cash necessities to move openly to support itself. Keeping down on paying, or in any case, storing cash forestalls the free progression of energy, and consequently the free progression of cash. For instance, we have seen various occurrences where people were reluctant to take care of the bills they owed until they originally got installments of cash because of them. Switching such a mentality can bring an unexpected plentiful positive reaction from life.

Assuming you surrender such perspectives and allow cash to circle, energy will stream, and life will compensate you with favorable luck, remembering the consistent progression of cash for your bearing. This is the verification of the inconspicuous rule of "internal-external correspondence"; for example, life considers the external mental condition inside yourself. If you make your sentiments or perspectives more certain, for example, defeating a reluctance to take care of a bill or the storing of cash, life outwardly will answer decidedly to you in kind.

Frequently the people who experience the ill effects of cash issues have acquired before and have neglected to reimburse, in any event, whenever they had the chance to do as such.

It is additionally essential to gather all cash owed to you, including the minutest of aggregates. Assuming that you do as such, cash will out of nowhere come to you from all bearings.

There are conditions where cash won't come in your direction until you deal with dismissed parts of your life. When you offer those regions enough consideration, cash or other favorable luck can momentarily come in your direction.

www.ingramcontent.com/pod-product-compliance
Lightning Source LLC
Chambersburg PA
CBHW072129150726
47999CB00005B/2211